A PORTRAIT OF
SHEFFIELD

PETE HILL

HALSGROVE

First published in Great Britain in 2005

Title page: Telegraph House.

British Library Cataloguing-in-Publication Data
A CIP record for this title is available from the British Library

ISBN 1 84114 381 2

HALSGROVE
Halsgrove House
Lower Moor Way
Tiverton, Devon EX16 6SS
T: 01884 243242
F: 01884 243325
email: sales@halsgrove.com
website: www.halsgrove.com

Printed and bound by D'Auria Industrie Grafiche Spa, Italy

Introduction

It was a cold, grey, rainy afternoon in January, and I was hard at work on a particularly tedious, difficult studio shoot when I got the phone call. A polite gentleman who turned out to be Roly Smith, Editorial Manager of Halsgrove Publishing, enquired if I had any stock shots of Sheffield. Any excuse to take a break from making minute adjustments to cutlery was welcome, so I got talking to him.

Roly explained he was looking to put together a book which was to be called a *Portrait of Sheffield*, and was having difficulty finding suitable material. He'd recently received one of the regular mail shots I send out, so wondered if I had anything suitable.

The idea of being out and about rather than stuck in the studio seemed particularly appealing at that moment, so I was quite intrigued, and I rather rashly offered to shoot the book for him. When I realised what I'd said and the enormity of what I'd taken on, I quickly began to backtrack. However as he explained that my name would appear on the cover, and the choice of subject matter was entirely up to me, vanity took over, and I was hooked.

A week or so later, Roly phoned to give the go-ahead, and told me the publishers wanted all the photographs by the end of May, so the book could be published in the autumn. That gave me just over five months to shoot 150-plus finished, final shots. Thirty shots a month may not sound a lot, but I'm a very busy commercial photographer, and obviously earning my living has to come first. However, for aesthetic reasons, the light early in the morning, or late in the afternoon, gives a more pleasing result, so I could work around other assignments.

So began a series of very early, often freezing cold, escapades round Sheffield. I would research locations during the day, then work out the best time to come back from a lighting and activity point of view.

Sheffield is the UK's fourth largest city, and like many others, is changing fast. Hardly a week goes by without an old building disappearing or a new one being built. The city skyline is dominated by cranes, whether it's new offices, apartments or factories, and something seems to be always going up...or coming down.

I set out to capture a few brief months in the life of this fast-moving and cosmopolitan city. I wanted to remember the old Sheffield and to celebrate the new in a series of unusual photographs. And I've tried throughout to try to come up with something different; places that are less well-known, or shot in a different way.

Inevitably, this is a far from complete portrait. Some of the shots I initially intended to shoot I never got round to, some didn't work out as anticipated, and space is obviously limited. However I hope you enjoy this photographer's view of the place that used to be known as the Steel City – the place I am proud to call home.

Pete Hill
www.petehill.demon.co.uk

Very early on a very, very cold Sunday morning in January, dawn breaks over the east end of Sheffield, as the lights on Meadowhall's roof twinkle in the distance.

Taken from the same viewpoint as the previous shot on the hillside at
Wincobank, looking back towards the city centre.

A Supertram speeds by. You can see the frost on the track ballast.

The moon is still high in the sky, as the still canal acts as a perfect mirror.

A row of narrow boats tied up at Tinsley Locks. You can just
see the famous cooling towers in the distance.

Smoke rises from the chimneys of boats moored at Victoria Quays.
That's the canal basin to older readers, including myself.

Evening traffic rushes past the Millennium Galleries.

Sheffield Hallam University. I really like shooting buildings at dusk. You have only a short time to get the right effect. The sky really needs to be just the right shade.

The Crucible and Lyceum Theatres. A shame one of the bulbs in the streetlight is out.
This was shot the same week as an episode of the BBC2 *Culture Show*
was filmed in Sheffield, and they had the same problem.

Dusk at the Winter Gardens. Another cold wait for the sky to reach the right tone;
I shot a whole memory card of images, and this was the last frame.

A lone office worker is still hard at it late into the evening.

The towering monolith of the Royal Hallamshire Hospital. I think this must be
one of the ugliest buildings in Sheffield, dominating the skyline.

A few students make their way into Sheffield University's Students' Union.

The evening rush hour on Western Bank. The building has recently
been renamed the Richard Roberts Building.

After a long day at work, weary workers catch the Supertram home to Gleadless Townend.

The imposing flats at the top of St Phillip's Road. A few lights remain
on in the Arts Tower, as trams and traffic race by.

The evening traffic flows freely round Park Square roundabout as a tram zooms across the viaduct.

Taken on the same evening as the previous picture. I kept alternating
shots either side of the same footbridge. A few of the old colour Mainline
buses make their distinctive yellow and red streaks.

The evening rush hour traffic flows freely along the Parkway.

The same shot as the previous picture, this time in daylight.
This is a sight all too familiar to Sheffield's morning commuters.

A very cold, clear morning view of the city from Owler Bar. The tower on the horizon belching steam is the Ferrybridge Power Station, over 30 miles away.

Another long shot of the city, this time taken from the moors above Ringinglow.

A Sunday morning shot of the once award-winning Gleadless Valley estate.

Greystones viewed from the top of Psalter Lane.

During a cold snap, the residents of Norton Farm are warm inside their apartments.

A Highland cow in Graves Park seems less than impressed by the snow.

A typical Sheffield view. A row of dormer windows on terraced houses in Walkley.

A familiar sight to evening commuters in the west of Sheffield.
The serried ranks of the terraced houses of Hunter's Bar, from Brocco Bank.

Another early start on a Sunday morning was required to capture
the melting frost in the churchyard of St Nicholas, at High Bradfield,
below the moors on the western extremity of Sheffield.

This shot was taken just a few minutes later, on the way home for a well-deserved breakfast.
This farm stands in the picturesque Bradfield valley.

The Sheffield Alliah Mosque, in Roundell Street, Darnall.

A peaceful scene of urban dereliction, mirrored in the canal.

Another eerie reminder of Sheffield's industrial heritage.

A hidden gem. I love the walk along the canal towpath, which is usually deserted apart from the anglers.

The moon sets behind the familiar bulk of the Forgemasters
building on the way to Meadowhall.

Another beautiful old building from Sheffield's industrial past, this time on the River Don.

A fascinating building I'd never come across before I started working on the book,
in South Parade, Shalesmoor. Shame about the modern windows on the ground floor.

The familiar Green Lane Works building near Kelham Island Museum. It is soon to be converted into luxury apartments, now that production in the factory has switched to Eastern Europe.

A couple enjoy a stroll in Cornish Place, which was one of the first conversions of old industrial buildings to apartments.

An interesting light fitting in front of the Globe Works at Shalesmoor.

The original wooden name sign of Cotton Mill Row, near Kelham Island.

Round the corner, local graffiti artists spray the wall in a more contemporary style.

As the refurbishment of the city centre continues apace, the skyline has become dominated by cranes. Here the finishing touches are put to yet another block of new apartments.

Only a few yards away, the dilapidated splendour of this 1930 Art Deco building is left to rot.

Castle House, another magnificent old building which I understand is to be converted into apartments.

From a completely different era, Sheffield Castle was the enforced
'home' of Mary Queen of Scots between 1570 and 1584.

I first came across this magnificent old building when shooting photographs about drug addiction among Asian youths. The ground was littered with syringes and tin foil.

A close up of Hammerton Street School. I tried shouting to get all the pigeons to fly away together, which would have made a stunning shot. However they remained totally indifferent to my pleas.

A beautiful half-timbered building on Haymarket. The modern
banner is a sign of the times for this area of Sheffield.

A reminder of Sheffield's past reputation as the capital of the 'Socialist
Republic of South Yorkshire'. I'll be watching you.

I like the contrast between the old and the new in this shot. The rows of windows in
the old 'little mesters' buildings are echoed in the modern office windows.

The Roebuck Tavern seems engulfed by the new Town Hall offices.

The brutally-modern yet amusingly-named Persistence Works,
home to The Yorkshire Artspace. How apt!

Yet another pub contrasted with modern offices. Here is The Red
Deer and the new university buildings on Pitt Street.

An unusual view of the city centre on a clear spring morning.
A Supertram hurries workers and shoppers towards Meadowhall.

The very first shot taken for this book.
Yet another new office building rises
above the Peace Gardens.

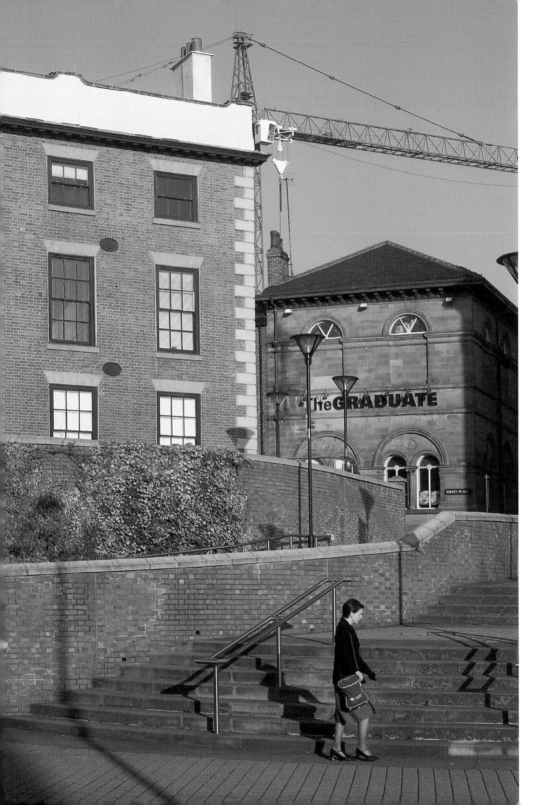

A lone office worker hurries to work.

Yet another crane on Sheffield's skyline. Here new flats being built on Campo Lane rise behind a well-known Sheffield building.

The early morning sun catches Telegraph House, once home to the local newspaper. The interesting roof line has a definite Eastern European feel.

I struggled to come up with something different photographically with one of
Sheffield's most distinctive new buildings, the Winter Gardens. Here the beautiful
parabolic larch roof arches make an almost abstract pattern.

The stunning facade of this old building hides modern offices behind. Some may
think this is desecration, but I think the architect has been quite sympathetic.

The sun reflected off the gold tinted windows of one of Sheffield's
most prestigious office buildings, Fountain Precinct.

Early evening sunlight catches on one of the most distinctive buildings on West Street.
The hardest thing about this shot was avoiding all the Supertram cables.

One of the best-known pubs on West Street, and a frequent haunt of mine in the early '80s. They used to have live bands upstairs, and it was very handy for the infamous Limit Club just down the road.

The Georgian elegance of Paradise Square, once home to much of the city's legal profession. Many have moved on to larger more modern premises elsewhere in the city.

Known to most people as the Manpower Services Commission building,
and hated for the way it blocked off one end of The Moor, this monolithic, red-brick
building is now home to the Department for Work and Pensions.

Victoria Hall on Norfolk Row, designed by local architect William Hale
and opened in 1908. It was described by Pevsner as 'free neo-baroque'.

The 1930s' old Fire Station on Division Street, now home to a bar not suprisingly called Central Fire Station.

A sight I used to see several times a day when I used to have to drive into town
to get my film processed. The 1970s flats at the bottom of Ecclesall Road.

The monolithic block of new apartments West One, overlooking Devonshire Green.

I'm sure many motorists will have seen this piece of stainless steel artwork, but can they think where? Called *Made in Sheffield* and created by Amanda King, it's just through the Wicker Arches, as you go out of town towards Meadowhall.

This stunning stainless steel sundial by Wendy Taylor commemorates
Harry Brearley, the inventor of stainless steel, near Don Valley Stadium.

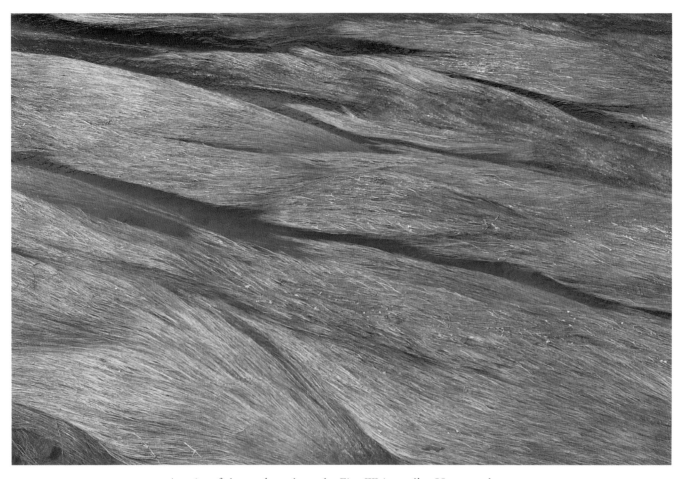

A series of shots taken along the Five Weirs walk. Here weeds are
teased into an abstract design by the flow of the River Don.

Nature always wins. Ivy reclaims an otherwise austere brick wall.

The Albion factory, or 'Tommy Wards' as my father used to call it.

The still River Don at Sanderson's Weir reflects an impressive tree.

Victoria Quays on a much warmer spring morning. I can vaguely remember being taken down here by my father as a small boy to visit a friend of his who was building his own boat.

During a morning break, a worker sneaks out for a bit of fishing.
Many engineering businesses still occupy canal-side workshops.

A couple of regional network trains meet on a viaduct over Levenson Street.

A modern Intercity train hurtles through the East End legacy of
Sheffield's past towards the gleaming modern city in the distance.

The East End is now home to some of the best sports facilities in the country, partly as a legacy of the 1991 World Student Games. Here Ice Sheffield glows in the deepening dusk.

Just across the road, The Institute of Sport is a hive of activity.

Don Valley Stadium. Here seen at the finale of Channel 4's reality TV show
The Games, which seems to have become a regular event.

For the last thirty years, the Crucible Theatre has been the
venue for the Embassy World Snooker championship Here technicians
put the final touches to the set the day before the first match.

Owlerton Stadium is the venue for regular speedway and greyhound
racing.   The roar of bikes revving-up fills the night.

The car park of the Hallam FM Arena is turned into a stables during the Festival of the Horse.

I have to confess I'm not a football person, but the game is such a large part of many peoples lives, a book about Sheffield has to show both grounds. Here Bramall Lane, the home of Sheffield United ('The Blades') is seen from the aptly-named Sky Edge.

Hillsborough, the home of Sheffield Wednesday (or 'The Owls'),
as seen from a hilltop overlooking the ground. In both shots you get
an idea of how Sheffield is cradled by the surrounding wooded hillsides.

By the time you read this, the City Hall should have reopened after its
lengthy refurbishment. Here the Oval Hall is getting a new floor.

A downstairs foyer is restored to its original 1930s' splendour by artists meticulously applying silver leaf.

Castle Market has some of the finest fresh fruit, meat and fish stalls, often overlooked by the majority of the population. The smell is divine, just like being by the sea.

As a child I used to love being taken here by my mother. A real treat
was a little plate of fresh cockles, with lots of salt and vinegar.

At Sheffield's commercial radio station, Hallam FM, Big John@breakfast shares
a joke with producer James and the Stuntman during the breakfast show.

Later in the day, things are all together more serious
as Rony Robinson at BBC Radio Sheffield interviews a guest.
The screen in the foreground offers Rony a few helpful tips.

Since it opened in 1996, Nonna's on Ecclesall Road has become a part of
Sheffield life. Front of house all is cool, calm and collected.

Meanwhile in the small kitchen, chef Nick Long frantically prepares for the lunchtime service.

The Cutlers' Hall is the premier venue for the meeting of the great and the good in Sheffield. Here finishing touches are made before an evening dinner dance.

At the other end of the culinary spectrum, David Fung busily serves
up tasty food for the residents of Sheffield Lane Top.

At the Fire and Police Museum, a rather bored looking officer guards the front desk.

This is obviously to deter would-be thieves tempted by
their fine collection of vintage fire extinguishers.

A proud father plays follow-my-leader with his daughter in Firth Park.
The row of houses facing the park always reminds me of Rustlings Road,
overlooking Endcliffe Park, though I imagine the prices are a little different.

I think this one speaks for itself. An old roadside marker, also in Firth Park.

Near the cathedral stands the statue of James Montgomery,
noted journalist, political activist and writer of hymns.

The statue of Queen Victoria in Endcliffe Park. Originally standing at the junction of Leopold Street and Fargate, it was moved to the park in 1930.

Sharrowvale Road at Hunters Bar. This area is synonymous in my mind with being
very right on and politically correct – and for the difficulty in finding
somewhere to park. Somehow that seems a bit of a contradiction.

A close up of the whole food shop, Down to Earth. Adverts for holistic therapy,
Feng Shui basics, acupuncture and practical philosophy abound.

Sunday morning in Endcliffe Park. A venue for football kick-abouts, bouncy castle, the kids playground...

... and tea at the café.

A magnificent terrace of houses on Ashdell Road, Broomhill. I think
most of them are now student bed sits, though I may be wrong.

Once the poshest hotel in Sheffield, still known to many as The Hallam Tower,
it was later renamed The Post House. It is now closed.

The traditional fruit shop in Old Fulwood village.

A tempting range of fine foods seen through the window of The Ranmoor Deli.

The Ranmoor Inn, with one of the prettiest churches in Sheffield, St John's.

St Mary's Church, Ecclesfield, seen rhrough spring blossom.

Early morning sun catches the etched windows of the Old Horns Inn, at High Bradfield.

The evening light glows through the windows of the Old Crown Inn on London Road.

A pleasant walk to work. The Royal Hallamshire Hospital looms through the spring blossom.

In the heart of Broomhall, once notorious as the drug and red light district,
but where today residents have created an oasis of calm.

Sheffield has to be be of the greenest cities in England, with so many tree-lined roads and parks. Here we see spring blossom on trees at Norton.

Another typical scene from the suburbs. Rows of bay-windowed, 1930s' semi-detached houses.

Spring comes late to one part of Ecclesall Woods, the scene of many childhood exploits.

Bluebells abound through the dappled shade.

A walk up the Limb Valley, towards Ringinglow, provided this idyllic scene.

Allotments, once a vital part of steelworkers' nourishment, arc now becoming very trendy. Here is the view from Gleadless, looking towards Meersbrook.

The newly-refurbished Botanical Gardens. Here a father and his daughters admire the view and the new fountain.

Springtime in the Botanical Gardens. A young family feed the birds among falling blossom.

A elderly couple enjoy a Sunday morning stroll past the main pavilion.

I remember being taken to Abbeydale Industrial Hamlet by my father just
before they started the renovation. It is seen here reflected in the lake
which provided the water power for the tilt hammers.

Every true Sheffielder loves their Henderson's Relish. As a child I had it on just
about everything. The joke was: 'Would you like some food with your relish!'

Printing company Polestar have invested over £100 million building a state of the art plant on part of the old Avesta site on Shepcote Lane. Here two of the enormous presses can be seen in the distance.

Many Sheffielders still prefer to stick to the city centre for their shopping. Lunchtime shoppers bustle on Fargate, while in the distance, a bus zooms up High Street.

Others, and many more from further afield, prefer the retail splendour of Meadowhall.

In the middle of the busy roundabout, Hunters Bar remains a small oasis of calm..

Further along Ecclesall Road, springtime shoppers enjoy the sunshine while browsing the upmarket shops.

At night London Road becomes a neon-lit mass of restaurants, while the ziggurat of
the Department of Work and Pensions looms over all.

A quite recent development on London Road is the proliferation of noodle bars. Friday night diners enjoy a cheap, delicious bowl.

The Forum is an Aladdin's Cave of goodies for the student and 'alternative' crowd.
The Gaudiesque outdoor eating area is a clever addition.

Sheffield has a well-founded reputation for its night life. Drinkers
queue behind the velvet rope on Devonshire Street.

A couple of takes on a quintessential English scene. Youngsters enjoy a game of cricket at Low Bradfield....

…while an older set enjoy a game at a more commercialised Park Head.

How better to end than with a new Sheffield beginning.
The traditional throwing of the bouquet.